Romance—the long-lasting type—starts with good communication. Trouble is, life sometimes gets in the way. A national survey recently disclosed that most married couples spend only three to four minutes in meaningful conversation daily. They spend the remaining 1,437 immersed in work, worries, parenting, play, sleep, hobbies, or watching TV.

Perhaps time isn't an issue for your marriage, but meaningful communication lags because one partner finds talking difficult. He or she honestly doesn't know what to say or ask.

Sometimes it suffers because we mistakenly think we know everything there is to know about each other. Or we settle for surface conversation rather than striving for deeper talk that connects our hearts.

My husband and I knew each other only six weeks before he proposed. Ours was a long-distance, five-month engagement. We married on February 20, 1982, took a three-week honeymoon, and then headed for a missionary career in Nepal.

Our first home was a mud and rock hut with a thatch roof. No electricity. No running water. Isolation and stress glued us together. Television and technology were nonexistent where we lived, so we spent evenings playing Scrabble and reading aloud. Circumstances taught us quickly how to communicate beyond surface stuff.

Three years later we returned to North America, and life started getting in the way. We discovered that meaningful communication took a lot more intentionality than before. So we began going on regular dates and asking each other creative questions, and these became some of our favorite activities.

Thanks to questions, we're still discovering gems about each other, and we always have something engaging to talk about. We stash questions in the glove compartment of our car and discuss them when we drive. We keep them in our bedside table so we can consider one or two before bedtime. We take them on dates and even when we visit a hotel hot tub.

I encourage you to do the same with this little book. May you enjoy these questions, and may your romance be the long-lasting type.

Cheering for your marriage,

Grace

www.gracefox.com

If you could remodel any room in our house, which one would you choose? Describe the completed look, including furniture.

List three free and simple
activities you enjoy.
What free and simple activities
do we enjoy together?

How can we do them more often?

6

To what biblical character would you
liken yourself? Why?

If you were to do a random act of
kindness for someone today,
what would it be?
Why?

If your friends gave you an award,
what would it be?

Isaiah 40:31 says God promises
renewed strength to those
who wait on Him.

Describe a situation in which you
experienced God's strength.

What did that look like?

~ ✺ ~

What part of your body
do you like most?

What part of my body
do you like most?

~ ✺ ~

If you could live anywhere in the world,
where would it be? Why?

If you could meet any person from
history, who would it be? Why?

*

"You can turn painful situations around through laughter. If you can find humor in anything, even poverty, you can survive it" (Bill Cosby).

Describe an experience in which humor lessened pain or lightened a heavy load.

*

Describe the best Christmas present you received as a child.

Describe the ideal vacation
for our family (money and time
being no object).

Where would we go? What would we
do? How can we simulate it while
staying within our means?

Complete this sentence: The quality I
appreciate most about you is…

Describe the ultimate romantic
getaway. Where would we go?
What would we do?

What's the last creature comfort you'd
want to give up?

Erich Segal wrote in the 1970 movie
Love Story, "Love means never having
to say you're sorry."

Do you agree? Why or why not?

What would you do if you had one
evening a week to spend on yourself?

What is your greatest fear? What can I
do to help you face that fear?

*

Who has taught you a valuable life lesson, and what was it?

*

What comes to mind when you think about our growing old together?

If you could design a new house for our family (money being no object), what unique features would it contain?

Why did you choose these features?

What was our most romantic date so far?
What can we do to create another ultra-
romantic memory?

What's your favorite board game? Why do you enjoy it more than others?

What's one thing you hope God won't
ask you to do?

~&

What impression do you want people to
have of us as a couple?

What actions must we take to ensure this
happens and is a true impression?

~&

If you could effortlessly learn a
foreign language, which one would you
choose? Why?

Someone said, "When I stopped thinking about what I wanted from God and started focusing on what God wanted from me, my life got better."

What's your response to that? What do you think God wants from you?

What's your favorite warm-weather activity? Describe a good memory associated with it.

What do you consider the most
important action needed to divorce-proof
our marriage?

Describe your favorite childhood
Christmas tradition. What's your
favorite tradition now?

What's your favorite piece of furniture in
our home? Your least favorite?

Recall your most embarrassing
situation as a teen.

Describe an experience that caused you
to question a long-held belief.

If you could meet any biblical character, who would it be? Why? What question would you ask him or her?

Recall your most memorable
Christmas. How old were you? What
made it more memorable than others?

George Bernard Shaw said, "A happy
family is but an earlier heaven."

How can we make our home
a heaven on earth?

᠅

Tell me how you learned to drive.

Who taught you? What (mis)adventures
did you have?

᠅

What's your greatest concern right now
for our family? What can I do to help
ease that concern?

～

Describe a teacher or coach who made
a positive impact on your life.

～

❦

Take turns listing things for which
you're grateful.
Make this an ongoing list.

❦

❧

What do you consider the perfect age?
Why?

❧

Recall our wedding day. What was the highlight for you?

What environmental issue concerns you
most? What can we do about it as a
couple or family?

～

What's the most memorable marriage
advice you've received?

～

*

"Think big thoughts but relish small treasures" (H. Jackson Brown Jr.).

What big thoughts are in your heart?
What small treasures do you relish most?

*

Make up an acronym of my name, each letter representing a positive character quality that describes me.

Name three things that would be high on
your bucket list.

What's your most productive time of day? What tasks do you like to accomplish during that time?

❦

What aspect of God's character
means the most to you?

Why did you choose this one?

❦

If you could carve four faces on Mount Rushmore, whose faces would you choose? Why?

~

What would you like to do to celebrate
our next anniversary?

~

Proverbs 19:21 says we can make many plans but the Lord's purpose prevails.

Describe a time when you made plans but God directed otherwise.

What was the outcome, and what did you learn through this?

What comes to mind or what emotions
do you feel when you think of
white-water rafting?

If you could go back to school and upgrade your education, what studies would you pursue? Why did you choose those studies?

What was one of the most difficult
days of your life so far?

What helped you cope?

Name a book or movie that impacted
your life. Describe the impact.

If you could write a book about marriage, what would the topic be? What would the title be? Why would you choose this topic?

Tell me a story—funny or otherwise—
from your high school days.

~

What dreams do you have for our
retirement years?

~

$\backsim$

Describe the most amazing answer to
prayer you've personally experienced.

$\backsim$

⬦

"Courage is being afraid but going on anyhow" (Dan Rather).

What promise from God's Word instills courage in you when you feel afraid?

⬦

～

What legacy do you want to leave as an
individual? As a couple?

～

The fruit of the Spirit is love, joy, peace, patience, kindness, goodness, faithfulness, gentleness, and self-control.

Which of these qualities do you most appreciate in me?

Give examples of how you've seen these demonstrated.

We're marooned on a desert island with no electronic devices! How would you like to pass the time?

❦

What three values do you believe are
nonnegotiable for our marriage?

❦

Name one person who has played an
influential role in your life.
Explain that role.

～

What's your favorite Bible story?
How has it impacted your life?

～

Recall a humorous experience from our
marriage that showed the difference
between the way men and women think.

&

Recall your most embarrassing
situation as an adult.

&

Which vacation experience would
you prefer—lying on a tropical beach,
camping in the woods, seeing
Disney World, visiting family, or
mountain climbing? Why?

To which continent would you travel if
money were no obstacle? Why?

What sights would you like to see there?

What one man-made object would most
improve your life, and why?

What's the goal, or bull's-eye, for our marriage? How can we ensure we hit the bull's-eye?

Tell me a funny story from your
elementary school days.

If we were to go on a shopping spree this weekend and you could buy anything you wanted, what store would you visit? What would you buy there?

Jesus said we're to forgive those who sin against us. Describe a situation in which you forgave someone. How did doing so impact you?

If you could own a vanity license plate,
what would it say? Why?

✑

"Let us have the courage to do what God wants even if it is difficult" (Mother Teresa).

What's the most difficult thing God has asked you to do?

What did you learn from it?

✑

What would be the ideal way to
celebrate your next birthday?

Congratulations! You've been selected to appear on the game show of your choice. Which show do you choose? Why?

Complete this sentence: The thing that
first attracted me to you was…

What piece of electronic equipment
in our house do you appreciate most?
Why?

What's the glue that holds us together?

What household chore do I do that you appreciate most?

If you received an invitation to a masquerade party, what costume would you choose for yourself? What costume would you choose for me? Why?

If you could take a cruise, where would
you go? Why? How long would that
cruise be?

What is your top priority this week?
How can I help you achieve it?

If we were to go on a two-week
ministry trip, where would you choose
to go? What type of ministry would you
like to do?

If you could choose an era in which to be born, which one would you choose? Why?

How do you think we're doing at
expressing our love for each other in
front of our kids?
If there's room for improvement, what
specific things can we do?

How did your family acknowledge
Easter when you were a child?
What Easter traditions do you most
appreciate now?

Do you feel as if I'm helping you achieve your full potential? If not, what actions can I take to be more helpful?

Dream big! What wild adventure would you like to share as a couple?

What would it take to make it happen?

What marital advice would you give to a man engaged to be married? A woman?

If you could have any career you wanted, what would you do?

Recall a day you would like to redo.
What would you do differently?

If you could ask God any question you wish, what would it be, and why?

Tell me a funny story from your middle school days.

What is your love language—quality time, gifts, encouraging words, physical touch, or acts of service?

How can I best speak your language?

Tell me what brings you pleasure when we make love. Practice makes perfect!

"Courage doesn't always roar. Sometimes it's the quiet voice at the end of the day saying, 'I will try again tomorrow'" (Mary Anne Radmacher).

Have I displayed this type of courage? How?

Complete this sentence: You make me laugh when you…

Brainstorm ideas for wacky dates. Which two shall we do in the next two months?

Invent a sexy love story in which we're the main characters. Let's act it out!

Complete this sentence: Our love is like…

What weekly or monthly rituals do we share as a couple? Which ones do you enjoy or value the most?

What does romance look like to you in the midst of a busy schedule? How can we turn up the heat in our romance?

What's your favorite sitcom, present
or past? Why did (do) you enjoy it so
much?

Recall some of our firsts and favorites—
first kiss, first date, first vacation, favorite date, favorite honeymoon memory,
favorite "couple" activity…

⊷

What's your favorite Scripture verse?
Why is it so meaningful to you?

⊷

What type of service project can we do
as a couple either in our community at
large or in our neighborhood?

⊷

More Great Books by Grace Fox
from Harvest House Publishers

Peaceful Moments to Begin Your Day
In this lovely padded hardcover, Grace Fox invites you to delight in your faith by nurturing your relationship with God each day. In these encouraging devotions, you'll encounter inspirational stories, Scripture-based prayers, and engaging meditations that lead you to the grace, comfort, and wisdom of God's presence.

10-Minute Time Outs for You and Your Kids
Grace provides engaging stories, activities, and prayers in a welcoming format to help you lead your family to the riches of God's Word and sharing time together—in 10 minutes.

Morning Moments with God
Discover fresh biblical insights and renew your spirit as you savor more than 150 new devotions by Grace for women. These gems of godly wisdom focus on God's faithfulness and reflect on His power, presence, and promises in your life today.

Moving from Fear to Freedom
Grace demonstrates how you can face your fear and actually let it be a catalyst for change. She outlines "the upside of fear": When we stop hiding from God and instead cry out to Him for help, He answers, and we experience Him in new ways.

Tuck-Me-In Talks with Your Little Ones
Trade in a few of your bedtime stories for memory-making moments with this collection of fun conversation starters for kids ages three to eight. It's filled with open-ended questions that will stimulate your children's imagination and help them express their thoughts.

To learn more about Harvest House books and
to read sample chapters, visit our website:

www.harvesthousepublishers.com

HARVEST HOUSE PUBLISHERS
EUGENE, OREGON

Cover by Dugan Design Group, Bloomington, Minnesota

Cover illustration © chuwy / Getty

Published in association with The Steve Laube Agency, LLC, 5025 N. Central Ave., #635, Phoenix, Arizona 85012.

ONE-MINUTE ROMANCE FOR COUPLES
Copyright © 2015 Grace Fox
Published by Harvest House Publishers
Eugene, Oregon 97402
www.harvesthousepublishers.com

978-0-7369-5651-2 (pbk.)
978-0-7369-5652-9 (eBook)

Printed in the United States of America

14 15 16 17 18 19 20 21 / BP-CD / 10 9 8 7 6 5 4 3 2 1

ONE-MINUTE
ROMANCE
FOR COUPLES

GRACE FOX

HARVEST HOUSE PUBLISHERS
EUGENE, OREGON